Charles Dickens Presents

A CHRISTMAS CAROL

A full-length stage play

by Steven Young

Charles Dickens Presents A Christmas Carol, Copyright © 2020, **Steven Young**
All rights reserved.

CAUTION: Professionals and amateurs are hereby warned that performance of TITLE is subject to payment of a royalty unless written permission is given waiving such fee. The Play is fully protected under the copyright laws of the United States of America, and of all countries covered by the International Copyright Union (including the Dominion of Canada and the rest of the British Commonwealth), and of all countries covered by the Pan-American Copyright Convention, the Universal Copyright Convention, and the Berne Convention, and of all countries with which the United States has reciprocal copyright relations. All rights, including professional/amateur
stage rights, motion picture, recitation, lecturing, public reading, radio broadcasting, television, video or sound recording, all other forms of mechanical or electronic reproduction, such as CD-ROM, CD-I, DVD, information storage and retrieval systems and photo-copying, and the rights of translation into foreign languages, are strictly reserved. Particular emphasis is placed upon the matter of readings, permission for which must be secured from the Author in writing.

Anyone receiving permission to produce the Play is required to give credit to the Author as sole and exclusive Author of the Play on the title page of all programs distributed in connection with performances of the Play and in all instances in which the title of the Play appears for purposes of advertising, publicizing or otherwise exploiting the Play and/or a production thereof. Author's name must be one-third the size of the title.

ISBN: 978-1-943416-57-8
Published by Blue Moon Plays
1385 Fordham Road, Ste 105-279
Virginia Beach, VA 34764
Printed in the USA
Cover Concept by Gerald Young
Cover Design by Margaret McSeveney

CHARLES DICKENS PRESENTS
A CHRISTMAS CAROL

This script can be performed by community, educational, or professional theaters either for the stage, the classroom, or as reader's theater.

Copyright law prevents this script from being copied or shared by any technical or digital means.

If you wish to perform this play, you must do the following:

1. Purchase sufficient scripts for your performance :
   - Purchase a Multicopy PDF which allows you to print sufficient copies of this script (one for each cast member, plus 4 for the crew) at Blue Moon Plays. Click Return to Merchant to download your printable PDF. A link to the download will also be emailed to you, along with a link to the application for performance license.

   OR

   - Purchase sufficient printed hard copies (one for each cast member, plus 4 for the crew) - an automatic 10 percent discount is applied to multiple printed hardcopies at the point of ordering.
2. Apply for a performance license.
3. Pay a Performance Fee for the specific days of your performances.

All scripts and licenses shall be obtained at Blue Moon Plays at www.havescripts.com

If you wish to make changes in the script of any kind, you must receive permission from the publisher or the playwright. Permission is usually granted readily when schools or theaters face casting problems and the changes do not affect the quality or intent of the original.

For information, visit www.havescripts.com
email info@bluemoonplays.com or
call 757-816-1164

CAST LIST
60 roles to be performed using a cast of 20 or an unlimited number of actors

Charles Dickens-the author
Catherine Dickens-his wife
Boz-the oldest boy
Mary-the second child, the oldest girl and a lover of dolls
Kate-their third child and a nosey-Parker
Walter-their youngest offspring and a lover of ducks
Ebenezer Scrooge-a miser
Bob Cratchit-his clark
Fred-his nephew
Philanthropist 1-a thin deaf man
Philanthropist 2-a robust and charitable man
Caroler 1-the smallest of the quartet
Caroler 2
Caroler 3
Caroler 4
Jacob Marley-A ghost and former partner of Scrooge
Past-a ghost of memory and regret
Wisps-dancers and fragments of Scrooges memory
Boy Scrooge-Scrooge as a lonely grammar school student
Ian Todd-Scrooge's boyhood friend
Fan-Scrooge's delicate and loving sister
Mr. Fezziwig-a jolly former employer
Mrs. Fezziwig-his roly-poly wife
The Three Fezziwig Daughters: Millisep, Grenda, & Ufema-their giggling offspring
Dick Wilkins-a friend of nineteen and Scrooge's co-worker
Young Scrooge-Scrooge as an idealistic young man out in the world on his own
Lolly Sauscepan-a singer and a drinker
Bopsy Sue-a girl with a reputation and a singer
Kibble MacGee-a flirt and a singer

Belle-Scrooge's boyhood love
Adult Scrooge-a stern man of business
Lady Belle-the woman of great substance and Scrooge's passion
Angels-dancers and agents of past
Mr. Primm-a representative of a bank
Present-a ghost of the momentary and the now, embodying the generosity of giving
Mrs. Cratchit-wife of Bob and devoted mother
Peter Cratchit-a boy joker
Jack Cratchit-a boy tattle tale
Miranda Cratchit-a girl and lover of life
Gillian Cratchit-a sprite of a girl
Belinda Cratchit-a child older than her years
Martha Cratchit-the oldest teen who has learned the lessons of life
Tiny Tim-an invalid and child of sweetness
Gwendolyn-Fred's fiery wife
Topper-a bachelor and self proclaimed thespian
Ms. Gummage-Topper's love interest
Ignorance-a boy parasite
Want-a gnawing girl
Future-a ghost of death and condemnation
Mr. Chinfold-a large man of business consuming all in his path
Mr. Spry-a miserly skeleton of a man
Mr. Snuff-an abuser of substances
Old Joe-a syphilitic trader of used commodities
Laundress-a domestic
Undertaker-one who dabbles in death
Charwoman-a bold hag
Town Person-a man accosted in the streets by Scrooge
Daniel Doyce-an Irish grocery boy
Beggar Child-a starved singer
Ensemble-workers, singers, dancers and street people

NOTE:

A Christmas Carol requires many locales, which can be suggested with light pools and/or simple furniture pieces. While the story is imagined, the author's writing space is realistic. Dickens could be placed off to the side, but it is my suggestion the attic is raised making it the highest part of the set. All other action could take place below as if one descends into the story.

How the author is used is up to each company. He could be revealed writing and then read his work aloud as if in editing mode, or he could be inventing it aloud from his mind and end a section by putting it to paper. He can remain at his desk throughout the performance or exit where indicated. A case could be made for Dickens leaving the attic and stepping in an out of the flow of the novel, observing, but not interacting with the characters.

There are suggested moments for music. Each company is encouraged to add or subtract period or seasonal music as they see fit.

The Wisps and Angels can be double cast or performed by two separate sets of actors.

CHARLES DICKENS PRESENTS
A CHRISTMAS CAROL

ACT I

In the darkness we hear a mournful tune, eventually a BEGGAR CHILD is revealed singing. CHARLES DICKENS is at his desk in the attic of his home. The light cocoons him as if it is the writer's circle of attention. DICKENS appearance is disheveled. Pages are scattered about, books are piled on the shelves and his desk is cluttered. DICKENS rubs his unshaven face, pours a heavy dram from a bottle of whisky and downs it. As the song ends, the CHILD exits. DICKENS picks up a page reads it and then crumbles it.

DICKENS: Start of December—I've barely written a phrase. It's not writers block I suffer, it's an entire city wall of blocks. *(Laughs and tosses the page.)* My daughter's diary is more compelling. You call yourself a writer? Think—ah! Dickens your brain is bankrupt as the rest of your affairs. Can't afford a fourth literary disaster, come now, it's only three—no one in the world bothered to read <u>Martin Chuzzlewit</u> and therefore they have no idea they hate it. What idiot in the world agrees to finance the production costs of a novel they haven't finished and probably will not be published? *(HE pounds his head on his desk. A knocking at the door takes up the same rhythm, breaking the cocoon.)* I'm working!

CATHERINE (OFF): Is everything all right, Charles, I heard voices?

DICKENS: Talking to myself, Mrs. Dickens.

CATHERINE (OFF): Why on earth?

DICKENS: To be assured intelligent conversation. Now go away!

CATHERINE (OFF): As you wish!

DICKENS: I wish! *(Beat.)* There isn't a ghost of a chance of making the 19 December deadline. *(Pours a drink and toasts.)* To the death of the *dead*-line…dead, dead—wait a tick. *(He writes.)* Marley was dead: to begin with. There is no doubt whatever about that. Old Marley was as dead as a doornail. Mind! I don't mean to say that I know what there is particularly dead about a doornail. I might have been inclined to regard a coffin nail as the deadest piece of iron in the trade, but back to the point I started from. There is no doubt that Marley was dead. This must be distinctly understood or nothing wonderful can come of the story I am going to relate; therefore, permit me to repeat, emphatically, that Marley was as dead as a doornail! Door, door, door, doornail—doorbell—door-mouse—door—what!

> *(ALL the CHILDREN rush in. MARY carries her doll followed by a very pregnant CATHERINE.)*

CHILDREN (ALL): Papa! Papa! Papa!

DICKENS: Catherine, the children—please!

CATHERINE: Mr. Dickens, find a little patience in your heart, they're here to remind themselves what their father looks like. They miss him. You miss your father, don't you children?

CHILDREN (ALL): We miss you, papa.

DICKENS: I know what you're doing; Catherine, using the children to woo me from my work will not win the day.

CATHERINE: Are you joining us for supper?

DICKENS: Not hungry.

BOZ: Papa, we want you to sing carols with us.

WALTER: Quack!

MARY: My doll hurt its nose. Will you kiss it?

DICKENS: The doll is fine, Mary. Have mother kiss it.

WALTER: Quack!

KATE: Read us a story?

DICKENS: I'm busy Kate.

WALTER: Quack!

BOZ: You know what I want?

KATE: Wait your turn, Boz.

MARY: I want my doll's nubbly nose all better.

WALTER: Quack!

DICKENS: Walter, what are you doing?

WALTER: Quack!

BOZ: He's being a duck.

WALTER: Quack!

DICKENS: It's embarrassing; I'm a novelist and one of my own children refuses to speak the Queen's English. Walter, you cannot go through life relying on poultry as a means of communication.

WALTER: Quack, quack, quack, quack, quack!

BOZ: I can be a cow, look, moo.

(ALL the CHILDREN begin mooing.)

DICKENS: No livestock is permitted in these quarters.

CATHERINE: Charles, you've been at the page for three days. Locked away in the attic, you've neglected to eat, to sleep, or to be with your family. Something is wrong.

WALTER: Quack!

DICKENS: Wrong? That's an understatement; I have a child so perilously steeped in ignorance he can't speak and of those who can, I hear nothing but 'want.' Worse yet, you're belly is full with another child and we're drowning in debt.

CATHERINE: I believe you had a hand in my current situation.

DICKENS: We barely maintain house here in lovely Osnaburgh Terrace, I write in an attic and have never been less inspired than at this moment.

CATHERINE: Children, come with me. *(SHE ushers them aside.)* Your father is behaving like a squeezing—

wrenching, grasping, scraping, clutching, covetous old sinner.

DICKENS: Uh…Let me write that down.

CATHERINE: What has come over you, Charles?

(DICKENS wads up a piece of paper as the CHILDREN march about.)

DICKENS: Nothing! That's the problem. Nothing has come over me. I can't write. I can't think. I have a dead line I'm sure to miss. Nails, I'm stuck on—doornails. Stop that racket!

(The CHILDREN cling to their mother.)

CATHERINE: Charles, its nearly Christmas—

DICKENS: If I don't finish the manuscript there won't be a Christmas nor a house to have it in.

CATHERINE: America loved you when you toured the States, performing readings?

DICKENS: So much so they plagiarized my books lock-stock and binding. We won't see a pence for them. The legalities to protect my work came from my pocket and surpassed whatever we could have hoped to gain.

CATHERINE: Did you secure a Barrister?

DICKENS: His intelligence barely rivaled the pulp on which he wrote his briefs. Forgive me; I'm being extravagant in my praise of the fellow.

CATHERINE: Charles—

DICKENS: Damn Americans, I never suspected they would steal a book, truth be told, I was utterly amazed they could read.

CATHERINE: You've wanted to leave Chapman and Hall; this may be the time.

DICKENS: I owe them money and to get them to display any interest in the book I'm currently writing, I promised to cover the gap in sales. I've looked into Bradbury and Evans Publishing. They're a respectable enough literary firm.

CATHERINE: You've never mentioned them.

DICKENS: They're the chaps send 'round a turkey each Christmas, of course, I assume the afore mentioned bird is in no way metaphorical of how they conduct business.

CATHERINE: We'll find the money. Children, run along and play.

(The CHILDREN noisily chase about.)

DICKENS: How do you propose to 'find' money? Will we live on hope? Will hope meet the bills? We have creditors crawling over us. Look—bills for the dwelling, bills for the grocer, butcher bills, bills for dress fabric, bills for that ridiculous hat you bought at the milliners— *(The CHILDREN crash into the desk.)* That's it! Out. All of you out, out, OUT, OUT!!!

(The CHILDREN quickly exit. CATHERINE touches her stomach.)

CATHERINE: I felt a kick. I hope you're pleased; you even managed to scare the little Dickens.

DICKENS: You're as large as a donkey.

CATHERINE: Charles!

DICKENS: And you needn't bray like one.

CATHERINE: I carry your child.

DICKENS: Maybe we should look to decrease the surplus population.

CATHERINE: *(Beat.)* Even for you, that was particularly cruel. Do you intend to *screw* us all to the sticking post?

DICKENS: Starting with you my dear wife if you do not cease talking!

CATHERINE: You can be as cold as scrap iron in winter, Charles, like an old gnarled screw of no use to man or women. Goodnight you old…screw. *(Exits.)*

DICKENS: Humbug, you shrew! Shrew…screw—screwed…screw-id, scrod—Scrooge. *(Considers.)* Scrooge? Scrooge. Say, that's good. *(Writes.)* "Scrooge never painted out Old Marley's name. There it stood, years afterwards, above the warehouse door: Scrooge and Marley. Sometimes people new to the business called Scrooge Scrooge, and sometimes Marley, but he answered to both names. It was all the same to him.
   (Shift: Revealed are SCROOGE and CRATCHIT.)
Once upon a time – of all the good days in the year, on Christmas Eve – old Scrooge sat busy in his counting house. It was cold, bleak, biting weather: foggy withal: The

city clocks had only just gone three, but it was quite dark already: The fog came pouring in at every chink and keyhole, and was so dense without, that although the court was of the narrowest, the houses opposite were mere phantoms." *(DICKENS exits.)*

SCROOGE: …You ask how you can ever pay me the figure owed. That, sir, is none of my concern. You borrowed money, if you had no agenda for repaying it, then you are not a debtor, but a common thief. You will pay me your due by the very stroke of the clock agreed upon or you shall find yourself in a debtor's prison. Yours resolutely: Ebenezer Scrooge.

CRATCHIT: *(Writing.)* Eeeeebeneeeeeezer Scrooge, wishing to you and yours, a very merry Christmas—

SCROOGE: Cratchit!

CRATCHIT: *(Drops his papers.)* Quite sorry sir. *(Retrieves the papers.)*

SCROOGE: Never let me hear you utter that maxim again.

CRATCHIT: Yes, sir.

SCROOGE: Take heed of my warning.

CRATCHIT: Very good, sir.

SCROOGE: I will not be contradicted.

CRATCHIT: I promise never again to say, "Merry Christmas."

SCROOGE: Cratchit!

CRATCHIT: *(Drops the papers again.)* My fault, sir. *(HE retrieves the papers.)*

SCROOGE: I should say so. Back to work and not another word.

CRATCHIT: *(Fetches coal.)* Pardon me, sir.

SCROOGE: Where are you going?

CRATCHIT: To stoke the fire, sir.

SCROOGE: Why?

CRATCHIT: …It's out sir.

SCROOGE: Your point?

CRATCHIT: I'm cold, sir.

SCROOGE: Wear a coat.

CRATCHIT: A lump or two should do the trick.

SCROOGE: Do you provide the fee for the coal?

CRATCHIT: No, sir. *(Puts down the coal.)*

SCROOGE: Perhaps it's best you learn to make due. This isn't a Turkish bath. See to it those letters are posted before noon.

CRATCHIT: *(Grabs the mail.)* There won't be a delivery tomorrow, sir. It's Christmas—

SCROOGE: Cratchit!

CRATCHIT: *(Drops the mail, then whispers:)* ...day.

SCROOGE: I forbid you to mention it again. One more outburst—

FRED: *(Enters.)* Merry Christmas, Uncle!

SCROOGE: Ah! I am to be tormented with that cursed phrase!

FRED: God Save you, Mr. Cratchit!

CRATCHIT: Thank you, sir.

FRED: Please, call me Fred.

CRATCHIT: Thank you, sir—I mean Fred.

SCROOGE: There's a picture of sentiment, my nephew and my clark with barely a farthing between them.

FRED: Uncle, it is the season of good will.

SCROOGE: Bah! Humbug!

FRED: Christmas a humbug, uncle, surely you don't mean that.

SCROOGE: I do. What right have you to be merry?

FRED: Come, then, what right have you to be dismal?

SCROOGE: What reason have you to be cheerful?

FRED: What reason have you to be morose?

SCROOGE: You're poor enough!

FRED: You're rich enough!

SCROOGE: Bah! Humbug!

FRED: Don't be cross, uncle.

SCROOGE: What else can I be, when I live in such a world of fools as this Merry Christmas! Out upon Merry Christmas. What's Christmas time to you but a time for paying bills without money; a time for finding yourself a year older, but not an hour richer. If I could work my will, every idiot who goes about with "Merry Christmas" on his lips, should be boiled with his own pudding, and buried with a stake of holly through his heart!

FRED: Uncle—

SCROOGE: Nephew! Keep Christmas in your own way, and let me keep it in mine.

FRED: But you don't keep it.

SCROOGE: Let me leave it alone, then. Much good it has ever done you.

FRED: I have always thought of Christmas as a good time: a kind, forgiving, charitable, pleasant time: the only time I know of, in the long calendar of the year, when men and women seem by one consent to open their hearts freely, and to think of people below them as if they really were fellow-passengers to the grave, and not another race of creatures bound on other journeys. And therefore, uncle, though it has never put a scrap of gold or silver in my pocket, I believe that it has done me good, and will do me good; and

I say, God bless it.

CRATCHIT: *(Applauding.)* Well said, Mr. Fred—

SCROOGE: Let me hear another sound from you, Cratchit, and you'll keep your Christmas by losing your situation. You're quite a powerful speaker, nephew; I wonder you don't go into Parliament.

FRED: Don't be angry, uncle. Come, dine with us tomorrow?

SCROOGE: I'll see you in hell first.

FRED: But why, uncle, why?

SCROOGE: Why did you get married?

FRED: Because I fell in love.

SCROOGE: 'Because you fell in love.' Good afternoon.

FRED: I want nothing from you; I ask nothing of you; why can't we be friends?

SCROOGE: Good afternoon.

FRED: I am sorry, with all my heart, to find you so resolute. But I have made the trial in homage to Christmas, and I'll keep my Christmas humor to the last. So, a merry Christmas, uncle.

SCROOGE: Good afternoon!

FRED: And A Happy New Year! *(HE kisses SCROOGE on the cheek.)*

SCROOGE: Bah! Humbug!

CRATCHIT: Merry Christmas, Mr. Fred—

SCROOGE: Cratchit! *(CRATCHIT drops his papers.)* You're a fine one, fifteen shillings a week, and a wife and family, talking about a merry Christmas.

CRATCHIT: Indeed, sir. I'll finish and put on the kettle.

SCROOGE: Oh?

CRATCHIT: A cup would take away the chill.

SCROOGE: A delightful notion, does your shed-u-al permit?

CRATCHIT: *(Thinks.)* ...no? No, it does not.

SCROOGE: I'm pleased your mother wit is not as empty as your pockets.

> *(PHILANTHROPISTS 1 & 2 enter. PHIL 1 has an ear trumpet and speaks as if everyone shares his affliction.)*

PHIL 1: Scrooge and Marley's, I believe.

PHIL 2: Have we the pleasure of addressing Mr. Scrooge, or Mr. Marley?

SCROOGE: Addressing Mr. Marley would be of little pleasure; he's been dead these seven years.

PHIL 1: What's that you say?

PHIL 2: Mr. Marley is dead.

PHIL 1: His name is Harley Head?

PHIL 2: No, Mr. Marley is dead.

PHIL 1: There's barley in the bed?

SCROOGE: Marley is dead.

PHIL 1: I'm sorry for your loss Mr. Head.

SCROOGE: He died seven years ago…this very night.

(A clock chimes seven. ALL listen.)

PHIL 2: Yes, ah—we have no doubt his liberality is well represented by his surviving partner. At this festive season of the year, Mr. Scrooge, it is more than usually desirable that we should make some slight provision for the poor and destitute, who suffer greatly at the present time. Many thousands are in want of common necessaries; hundreds of thousands are in want of common comforts, sir.

SCROOGE: Are there no prisons?

PHIL 2: Plenty of prisons—

SCROOGE: And the Union workhouses are they still open?

PHIL 2: They are. I wish I could say they were not.

SCROOGE: The treadmill is still in operation?

PHIL 2: Too busy, sir.

SCROOGE: I'm glad to hear it.

PHIL 2: Under the impression that it scarcely would furnish Christian cheer of mind or body to the multitude, a few of us are endeavoring to raise a fund to buy the poor some meat and drink, and means of warmth. We choose this time, because it is a time, of all others, when want is keenly felt, and abundance rejoices.

PHIL 1: What shall we put you down for?

SCROOGE: Nothing.

PHIL 1: Very generous, Mr. Head—

PHIL 2: He wishes to remain anonymous.

SCROOGE: I wish to be left alone. I don't make merry myself at Christmas and I can't afford to make idle people merry. I help to support the establishments, I have mentioned: they cost enough: and those who are badly off must go there.

PHIL 2: Many can't go there; many would rather die.

SCROOGE: If they would rather die, they had better do so and decrease the surplus population. Good afternoon, gentlemen.

PHIL 2: Good afternoon, sir.

PHIL 1: I hope you fix your bed.

PHIL 2: Come along.

PHIL 1: Merry Christmas. Strange fellow that Mr. Head.

(PHIL 1 & 2 exit.)

SCROOGE: *(CRATCHIT stares in amazement.)* Close your maw. Those people are not my business. It's enough for a man to understand his own business and not to interfere with others. Mine occupies me constantly, as yours should you. Have I made myself clear?

CRATCHIT: Perfectly.

SCROOGE: Then back to work.

(CAROLERS 1-4 enter, singing. When finished, CRATCHIT applauds.)

CRATCHIT: Well done.

SCROOGE: Don't encourage them.

CAROLER 1: Might we have a halfpenny for our efforts, Governor?

SCROOGE: What would you do with it?

CAROLER 1: Buy sweets.

SCROOGE: I would think singing lessons would be in order.

CAROLER 2: My mum says we're the best carolers in the East End.

SCROOGE: Is that why she sent you across town to practice?

CAROLER 3: She says, "Practice makes perfect."

SCROOGE: Not in all cases.

CAROLER 4: We're hungry.

SCROOGE: Are you?

CAROLER 1: Yes, sir.

SCROOGE: I'm sure I have a chocolate.

CAROLER 2: Chocolate!

SCROOGE: Would you like some?

CAROLER 3: Can we have two?

SCROOGE: Certainly, would you like one in shiny paper tied up with a red ribbon? *(C-4 nods.)* Good, come here, little one. *(C-4 crosses to SCROOGE; HE leaps to his feet, ruler in hand, and chases CAROLERS 1-4 out.)* Out. All of you out, out, OUT, OUT! *(SCROOGE returns to his desk.)* What?

CRATCHIT: *(Dropping his papers.)* Nothing, sir. *(HE retrieves them and goes back to work. After a time, HE begins to hum a carol.)*

SCROOGE: I know what you're doing.

CRATCHIT: What?

SCROOGE: Be off.

CRATCHIT: It is after seven, sir.

SCROOGE: Go before my judgment gets the better of me.

CRATCHIT: *(Readies to leave.)* Thank you, sir—very much appreciated.

SCROOGE: You'll want all day tomorrow, I suppose?

CRATCHIT: If quite convenient, Sir?

SCROOGE: It's not convenient and it's not fair. If I was to stop you half-a-crown for it, you'd think yourself ill used; I'll be bound? And yet, you don't think me ill-used, when I pay a day's wages for no work.

CRATCHIT: Its only once a year, sir.

SCROOGE: A poor excuse for picking a man's pocket every twenty-fifth of December. But I suppose you must have the whole day. Be here all the earlier the next morning.

CRATCHIT: God bless you, Mr. Scrooge.

SCROOGE: Bah!

CRATCHIT: And a Merry Christmas, Mister—

SCROOGE: HUMBUG!

> *(CRATCHIT flees, slamming the door behind him. Shift: DICKENS is revealed. He reads from his pages.)*

DICKENS: Scrooge assembled his ledger of accounts and went home for bed. The Miser lived alone in the forlorn chambers that once belonged to his deceased partner, Jacob Marley. The yard became so dark that even Scrooge, who knew its every stone, was fain to grope with his hands. The

fog and frost so hung about that it seemed the Genius of the Weather sat in mournful meditation on the threshold.
(Shift: SCROOGE is revealed at his door.)
Now, it is a fact, that there was nothing at all particular about the knocker on the door, except that it was very large. It is also a fact, that Scrooge had seen it, night and morning, during his whole residence; then let any man explain to me, if he can, how it happened that Scrooge saw in the knocker, not a knocker, but Marley's face. *(Marley's face appears within the door.)*

SCROOGE: Ah! *(The face disappears.)* Humbug.

(SCROOGE exits. Shift: DICKENS in the writer's circle.)

DICKENS: Scrooge paused before he shut the door; and cautiously looked behind it. But there was nothing there except the ironwork that held it in place. He closed the door with a bang that resounded through the house like thunder. The darkness grew heavier. Up the stairs he went, not caring a button for that: darkness is cheap, and Scrooge liked it. But before he shut the heavy door to his bedchamber, he walked through his rooms to see that all was right. Quite satisfied, he closed his door and locked himself in, which was his custom; then double-locked himself in, which was not his custom. Thus secured against surprise, he put on his dressing gown, slippers, and his nightcap, and yet, the face of Marley, seven years dead, slipped past the deadbolt of reason to take residence in the master bedroom of his mind.

(Shift: SCROOGE enters his bedroom.)

SCROOGE: Where has the day gone? Time to close my eyes. *(Gets into bed.)* Ah, humbug.

(Silence.)

MARLEY (Off): Scrooooge!

SCROOGE: Yes? What is it? Who's there? I'm armed! I will give you this one chance to leave. *(Waits.)* Humbug.

MARLEY (Off): Scrooooge!

SCROOGE: I do not find this amusing! Humbug!

MARLEY (Off): SCROOOOOGE!!!!

SCROOGE: I'm not afraid of you. You're a coward. Show yourself, you humbug. *(MARLEY enters.)* Do I know you? *(MARLEY nods.)* Are you a ghost? *(MARLEY nods.)* Can you speak? *(MARLEY nods.)* Then do it!

MARLEY: *(Removes the bandage holding his jaw shut.)* Ah…

SCROOGE: What do you want with me?

MARLEY: Much.

SCROOGE: Who are you?

MARLEY: Ask me who I was.

SCROOGE: You're very particular, for a shade. Who were you then?

MARLEY: In life I was your partner, Jacob Marley.

SCROOGE: Jacob? Jacob Marley?

MARLEY: You don't believe in me.

SCROOGE: I don't.

MARLEY: Why do you doubt your senses?

SCROOGE: Because, a little thing affects them, an undigested bit of beef, a blot of mustard, a crumb of cheese, a fragment of an underdone potato. There's more of gravy than of the grave about you, whatever you are. You're humbug, I tell you; humbug.

MARLEY: AHHHHH!

SCROOGE: *(Goes to HIS knees.)* Mercy! Dreadful apparition, why do you trouble me?

MARLEY: Man of the worldly mind, do you believe in me or not?

SCROOGE: I do, Jacob, I do. But why do you come to me?

MARLEY: It is required of every man that the spirit within him should walk abroad among his fellowmen, and travel far and wide; and if that spirit goes not forth in life, it is condemned to do so after death. It is doomed to wander through the world and witness what it cannot share, but might have shared on earth and turned to happiness! Ahhh!

SCROOGE: You are fettered. Tell me why?

MARLEY: I wear the chain I forged in life. I made it link-by-link, and yard-by-yard; I girded it on of my own free will, and of my own free will I wore it. Is its pattern strange to you?

SCROOGE: Jacob, please—

MARLEY: *(Places the chain over SCROOGE'S neck and HE drops under the weight.)* Know the weight and length of the strong coil you bear yourself? Yours was full as heavy and as long as this, seven Christmas Eves ago. You have labored on it, since.

SCROOGE: Jacob, Jacob Marley, speak comfort to me, Jacob.

MARLEY: I have none to give. I cannot rest, I cannot stay, I cannot linger anywhere. AHHH! Mark me… *(Takes back the chain.)* In life my spirit never roved beyond the narrow limits of our money-changing hole; weary journeys lie before me.

SCROOGE: Seven years dead and travelling all this time?

MARLEY: The whole time. No rest, no peace—nothing but the incessant torture of remorse. No space of regret can make amends for one life's opportunities misused. Such was I. Oh, such was I.

SCROOGE: But you were always a good man of business.

MARLEY: Business? Mankind was my business. The common welfare was my business; charity, mercy, forbearance and benevolence, were, all, my business. AHHHH! Hear me, my time is nearly gone. I am here tonight to warn you that you have yet a chance and hope of escaping my fate.

SCROOGE: You were always a good friend to me, Jacob.

MARLEY: You will be haunted, by three Spirits—

SCROOGE: Is that the chance and hope you mentioned, Jacob?

MARLEY: It is.

SCROOGE: I think I'd rather not.

MARLEY: Without their visits, you cannot hope to shun the path I tread. Expect the first tomorrow, when the bell tolls one.

(A bell tolls.)

SCROOGE: Couldn't I take 'em all at once, and have it over, Jacob?

(A bell tolls.)

MARLEY: Expect the second on the next night when the bell tolls the same hour.

SCROOGE: But, Jacob—

(A bell tolls.)

MARLEY: The third upon the next night when the last stroke of twelve has ceased to vibrate. Look to see me no more. *(HE exits.)*

SCROOGE: Humbug! Hum-bug?

(Shift: DICKENS is revealed at his desk.)

DICKENS: Scrooge tried to gasp one more 'Humbug,' but stopped at the first syllable. And being, from the emotion he had undergone, or the fatigues of the day, or his glimpse of the invisible world, or the conversation with the ghost, or the lateness of the hour, being much in need of repose; he fell asleep upon the instant. When Scrooge awoke he endeavored to pierce the darkness with his ferret eyes. Abruptly, the bell of a neighboring church struck and Scrooge listened for the hour.

(Shift: A bell tolls, SCROOGE is revealed in bed.)

SCROOGE: What? That can't be. It can't be. One? It was past two when I went to bed. It isn't possible that I've slept through a whole day and far into the night. It isn't possible something happened to the sun, and this is the first stroke of the afternoon? *(Waits.)* No ghost. Humbug!

(PAST and the WISPS of Scrooge's memory enter, dance and whirl about. SCROOGE finally breaks away as the WISPS exit.)

SCROOGE: I demand to know who and what you are?

PAST: I am the Ghost of Christmas Past.

SCROOGE: Long past?

PAST: No, your past.

SCROOGE: What business have you here?

PAST: Your welfare.

SCROOGE: I think a good nights sleep would do far more for my constitution—

PAST: Your reclamation, then. Take heed.

SCROOGE: Humbug.

PAST: Rise and walk with me.

SCROOGE: I am mortal and liable to fall.

PAST: Bear but a touch of my hand and you shall be upheld in more than this.

(Shift: To DICKENS in the attic.)

DICKENS: The apparition put out its strong hand as it spoke and clasped him gently by the arm. Scrooge studied the strange figure that appeared like a child: yet not so like a child as like an old man, which gave him the appearance—

CATHERINE: *(Enters.)* Charles? Charles, you have a visitor.

DICKENS: Who is it?

CATHERINE: He gave me his calling card. I believe he represents a benevolence group.

DICKENS: Let me see. It's from the Printers Pension Society. How can I possibly fit them in? I am already doing a public lecture on behalf of the Hospital for the Consumption and Diseases of the Chest. I've done my bit. Send him on his way.

CATHERINE: I'll do my best. Almost time for church.

DICKENS: Now?

CATHERINE: It's the Christmas season; we always attend the choir concert at St. Paul's.

DICKENS: I've heard the choir a thousand times.

CATHERINE: The children are waiting.

DICKENS: Go without me.

CATHERINE: It's a tradition; the entire family is together.

DICKENS: I haven't the time nor the inclination.

CATHERINE: You've been at the bottle, haven't you?

DICKENS: If it sparks the creative muse, then so be it. *(HE stops then attempts reconciliation.)* Forgive me Catherine. This sort of writing is new to me, the previous works were all serials, this is a continuous novel and I'm finding it a bit of a rough go. Can you appreciate that?

CATHERINE: I merely wish to support you and kindly beg you to not snap at me.

DICKENS: You… *(Swallows his retort.)* I need to work. You may go.

CATHERINE: I hope you find solace in ink and paper.

DICKENS: They don't talk back.

CATHERINE: I don't know you anymore, Charles. The man I married would have jumped at the chance to be at holiday with his family. Since you've started writing there seems room only for your pen and ledger. Blame your work, but your heart knows better.

DICKENS: Nonsense, you're prone to exaggeration.

CATHERINE: Charles, if I leave do not expect to see the children or myself again.

DICKENS: You should try amateur theatricals; you have a gift for the dramatic. Are we done?

CATHERINE: Quite.

(SHE exits. HE picks up his pages and reads.)

DICKENS: Though the night air was biting, it would have been in vain for Scrooge to plead that the weather and the hour were not adapted to pedestrian purposes; that he was clad but lightly in his slippers, dressing gown, and nightcap—the Spirit's intent would not waiver. They rose: made towards the window, passed through the wall, and stood upon an open country road. The city had entirely vanished.

(Shift: To SCROOGE & PAST at a school.)

PAST: We've arrived.

SCROOGE: Spirit, why have you dragged me here?

PAST: Look about you, Ebenezer.

SCROOGE: Good Heaven.

(Several Grammar School STUDENTS, in a hubbub, enter and exit.)

PAST: Do you know this place?

SCROOGE: Know it? I was a boy here.

PAST: You remember then?

SCROOGE: This is where I was schooled. *(A school bell rings. STUDENTS stream past SCROOGE and exit.)* Bless me, I don't believe it! Wait! Wait for me. *(HE gives chase.)*

PAST: They cannot hear you, Ebenezer. They are but the shadows of the things that have been and have no consciousness of us.

SCROOGE: Is no one left?

PAST: One boy.

SCROOGE: *(BOY-SCROOGE enters and sits.)* Has he nowhere to go?

> *(Carriage bells signal an arrival. IAN TODD enters carrying travel gear.)*

IAN TODD: Well Ebenezer, my family has come to gather me for half term break. I'm off. *(THEY shake hands.)* Can you believe we have nearly a month at home away from boarding school? It will be a welcome change to sleep in my own bed again and eat proper food.

BOY-SCROOGE: I'll see you at the start of next term, Ian.

IAN TODD: If you need a lift, Ian Todd III of the Ian Todd family is at your service. *(HE bows.)* You can ride with us into London. We've room in the coach.

BOY-SCROOGE: No, a carriage should be round to take me home in a tick.

IAN TODD: Where's your travel bag?

BOY-SCROOGE: Oh, right. I'll run and get it. Thank you, Ian.

IAN TODD: You're quite sure about the lift, it's getting late?

BOY-SCROOGE: I don't need a ride from the boy with two first names, 'Ian Todd.'

IAN TODD: If I were to only have the one, I would prefer either to 'Ebenezer.'

BOY-SCROOGE: Ebenezer is a name with advantage, makes me a bit of a curiosity.

IAN TODD: I suppose the girls fancy it?

BOY-SCROOGE: Of course.

IAN TODD: You're sure you don't want to come along?

BOY-SCROOGE: My father is on the way—now go.

IAN TODD: Merry Christmas, Ebenezer.

BOY-SCROOGE: You as well.

IAN TODD: *(Starts to exit and stops.)* I know accommodations remain open, but you're not staying for the entirety of the break are you?

BOY-SCROOGE: Course not.

IAN TODD: You don't have to pretend.

BOY-SCROOGE: Go already.

IAN TODD: It's late. Take this to hold you. *(Gives HIM bread from his satchel.)*

BOY-SCROOGE: *(HE hugs Ian.)* Thank you.

> *(IAN exits. We hear carriage bells depart. Pause, BOY-SCROOGE eats a bit of bread.)*

SCROOGE: He's alone?

PAST: Children boarded at school are expected to return home for the holiday.

SCROOGE: My father wanted what was best; being on my own was meant to develop inner strength.

BOY-SCROOGE: *(Reads.)* "And in that region there were shepherds out in the field, keeping watch over their flock by night. And an angel of the Lord appeared to them, and the glory of the Lord shone around them, and they were filled with fear. And the angel said to them, "Be not afraid; for behold, I bring you good news of great joy which will come to all people; for to you is born this day in the city of David a Savior, who is Christ the Lord. And this will be a sign for you: you will find a babe wrapped in swaddling cloths and lying in a manger." And suddenly there was with the angel a multitude of the heavenly host praising God and saying, "Glory to God in the highest, and on earth peace among men whom he is pleased!"

(HE looks about then starts to exit. Enter FAN.)

FAN: Ebenezer?

BOY-SCROOGE: Fan?

FAN: I've come to fetch you. *(HE runs and hugs her.)* Why the tears, dear brother?

BOY-SCROOGE: I received father's post I thought I was to remain at school. What are you doing here? What's changed?

FAN: I have come to bring you home, dear brother, forever and ever. You will never have to return.

BOY-SCROOGE: How can that be?

FAN: Father spoke so gently to me one night when I was going to bed, that I was not afraid to ask him once more if you might come home. He said, "Yes, you should," and sent me in a coach to bring you home. We're to be together all Christmas long, and have the merriest time in all the world.

BOY-SCROOGE: He said I could leave?

FAN: Never to return here again.

BOY-SCROOGE: You can't mean that?

FAN: I do Ebenezer. Being home now is like living in heaven. *(THEY hug then exit.)*

SCROOGE: Dearest Fan.

PAST: Always a delicate creature whom a breath might have withered.

SCROOGE: She was never strong.

PAST: But she had a large heart.

SCROOGE: So she had. And all to soon went to heaven.

PAST: She died giving birth and had as I think children?

SCROOGE: One child.

PAST: Indeed, your nephew…your nephew, Fred?

SCROOGE: …I do not wish to speak of it. Lead me where you will, Spirit.

PAST: Take my hand, close your eyes and in an instant we shall be there.

(Shift: Dickens is at his desk.)

DICKENS: Scrooge seemed uneasy in his mind; and answered briefly, "Yes." Within the moment they left the school behind and now were in the busy thoroughfares of a city, where shadowy passengers passed and re-passed, where shadowy carts and coaches battled for the way, and all the strife and tumult of a real city were present. It was made plain enough, by the dressing of the shops that here too it was Christmas; but it was evening, and the streets were lit up. The Ghost stopped at a certain warehouse door and entered.

(Shift: The Fezzi factory. The ENSEMBLE, LOLLY, KIBBLE, BOPSY & the FEZZIWIG FAMILY enter.

THEY sing while making the place ready for a party.)

DICKENS: At the sight of an old Scottish gentleman, in a Welsh wig, cavorting about the room, Scrooge cackled as if he had gone mad.

(Dickens exits.)

PAST: Do you know this place?

SCROOGE: Know it, I was apprenticed here. By god, its old Fezziwig, bless his heart; it's Fezziwig, alive again!

FEZZIWIG: Oi, there, Ebenezer! Dick!

DICK: *(Enters.)* You called, Mr. Fezziwig?

SCROOGE: Dick Wilkins, to be sure. Bless me, there he is. He was very much attached to me, was Dick.

FEZZIWIG: Hilli-ho, Mr. Willkins, where is young Master Scrooge?

DICK: He is finishing the accounts, Mr. Fezziwig.

FEZZIWIG: Oi, Ebenezer—no more work to night

YOUNG-SCROOGE: *(Enters.)* I am almost finished, sir.

FEZZIWIG: Drop whatever you are doing, lad. We'll have no more of this. It's Christmas Eve, Dick. Christmas, Ebenezer! Let's have the room made ready and dancing and drinks before a man can say, "Jack Robinson!"

ALL: Jack Robinson!

FEZZIWIG: Hilli-ho and what-what! Lets have room here! Mrs. Fezziwig, where are the wee bogies?

MRS FEZZIWIG: Whom do you mean?

FEZZIWIG: *(ALL cheer and clap as FEZZIWIG'S verbosity grows.)* I mean the ankle-biters, the rag-a-muffins, the sprites, the wee-people of kidlen land, the snot nosed finger biters, the breech beetles, the little soldiers of gnome county, the perpetual eaters of sweets, the messy mouthed munchers, le petite persons, the biscuit quaffers, those that be knee high to a cricket bat, better know as the Fezziwig belching briskets of Britannia.

MRS FEZZIWIG: Oh, you mean the children?

FEZZIWIG: Aye, of Clan Fezziwig!

MRS FEZZIWIG: Children, your father needs you?

(The CHILDREN enter.)

ALL: God bless, Mr. Fezziwig.

FEZZIWIG: Thank you my little pork chops. Do you know what tomorrow is?

CHILDREN (ALL): Christmas day!

FEZZIWIG: Indeed it is my little buttery basted game hens. 'Tis the night before Christmas and almost time for you to shut your eyes—do you know what tradition you must fulfill before we send you off to slumber?

CHILDREN (ALL): We must dance.

(Music, the CHILDREN dance. ALL applaud.)

FEZZIWIG: Now—time for bed.

CHILDREN (ALL): Ahhhh!

FEZZIWIG: Tomorrow is Christmas.

CHILDREN (ALL): Yea!!

FEZZIWIG: Good night wee-ones. Pleasant dreams.

CHILDREN: Good night.

(The CHILDREN sing as they exit.)

MRS FEZZIWIG: Are you to dance with me, Mr. Fezziwig?

FEZZIWIG-DAUGHTERS: *(Giggling and clapping in unison.)* Dance with mama! Dance with mama!

FEZZIWIG: I will try and save a turn for you, Mrs. Fezziwig.

MRS FEZZIWIG: Only one? Shall I be forced to box your ears, Mr. Fezziwig?

FEZZIWIG-DAUGHTERS: *(Giggling and clapping in unison.)* Box his ears! Box his ears!

FEZZIWIG: I shall only dance with the most beautiful woman present, Mrs. Fezziwig.

MRS FEZZIWIG: And who would that be?

FEZZIWIG: Why you, of course, my dear Mrs. Fezziwig. *(THEY kiss.)*

ALL: Oooooh.

FEZZIWIG-DAUGHTERS: *(Giggling and clapping in unison.)* Papa kissed mama! Papa kissed mama!

FEZZIWIG: We need a song!

DICK: Lolly Saucepan, sing us a tune?

LOLLY: Aye, but I must be paid in grog and strong ale.

BOPSY SUE: You wouldn't sing without me, now would you Lolly?

LOLLY: Bring me a tankard, Bopsy Sue and warble your hearts content.

BOPSY SUE: Kibble McGee come join and make us three.

KIBBLE: I'm Kibble MacGee and sing for free, if I get a kiss from a fair lad-dee.

BOPSY SUE: What shall we sing?

MRS FEZZIWIG: A song of the season.

LOLLY: Can it be a drinking song?

BOPSY: She don't know no church songs—

KIBBLE: On account, her soul is in a lurch, since she never goes to church.

LOLLY: What? I've been there…once!

KIBBLE: Your baptism doesn't count.

(LOLLY, KIBBLE & BOPSY sing a bawdy song, applause.)

DICK: What ho, what cheer! To the man who gave us this party. A cheer, a cheer for Mr. Fezziwig!

ALL: God bless, Mr. Fezziwig!

FEZZIWIG: I want to thank you one and all. Thank you. *(FEZZIWIG burps prodigiously, ALL laugh and cheer.)* Excuse me, it seems as if Mrs. Fezziwig's punch has punched back at me! *(ALL laugh. FEZZIWIG trumpet-farts. Pause.)* Or behind me! Too much spiced rum cake! *(Laughter.)* You have worked very hard and Mrs. Fezziwig and myself thank you. Allow me to introduce my three very eligible daughters Grenda, Millisep, and Ufema. Aren't they beautiful! They are in need of a handsome young bachelor to take them a turn on the dance floor.

DICK: I'll dance with 'em all!

FEZZIWIG: There's a lad, Dick Wilkins. Marry one and I'll make you a partner.

FEZZIWIG-DAUGHTERS: *(Giggling and clapping in unison.)* Dick Wilkins will dance with us! Dick Wilkins will dance with us! *(THEY are in such a frenzy they swoon and faint away.)*

FEZZIWIG: They do this every year. Come claim 'em, Dick. All—Eat, drink and be merry. Fiddler—the Sir Rodger de Coverly!

(ALL dance.)

FEZZIWIG: All of this dancing has left me parched. Dear friends, there's punch and games in the parlor!

(ALL cheer and exit as BELLE enters. SHE removes her coat and bonnet.)

YOUNG-SCROOGE: Dick, come here.

DICK: What is it, Ebenezer?

YOUNG-SCROOGE: Who is that?

DICK: Where?

YOUNG-SCROOGE: The girl, there?

DICK: Her?

YOUNG-SCROOGE: She's breathtaking.

DICK: No she isn't.

YOUNG-SCROOGE: She is the most beautiful girl I ever laid eyes on.

DICK: That's my sister you're talking about.

YOUNG-SCROOGE: Introduce me.

DICK: Are you daft?

YOUNG-SCROOGE: With love.

DICK: I've never seen you like this?

YOUNG-SCROOGE: Please?

DICK: Alright then—

YOUNG-SCROOGE: But make it a proper introduction.

DICK: Right—

YOUNG-SCROOGE: Better yet, introduce me as your associate.

DICK: Right—

YOUNG-SCROOGE: Don't let on how I feel—

DICK: Right—Belle?

BELLE: Ah, dear brother, I didn't expect you. What is it?

DICK: See that bloke standing there?

BELLE: Yes.

DICK: He's taken a fancy to you.

YOUNG-SCROOGE: Dick!

(YOUNG-SCROOGE gives chase as DICK runs off. Offstage carols are sung.)

BELLE: Might I have a word, sir? Is it true, you've taken a fancy to me?

YOUNG-SCROOGE: I apologize.

BELLE: Are you inclined to send brash young men in your place to court?

YOUNG-SCROOGE: Of course not, he set out to make sport of me and you have fallen prey to his jest. My apologies.

BELLE: Pity, I'd rather hoped he came baring the truth.

YOUNG-SCROOGE: Pardon?

BELLE: I had hoped it was true.

YOUNG-SCROOGE: You did—do?

BELLE: As you say it was a jest—

YOUNG-SCROOGE: It's true—I swear, I, uh…I wanted an introduction.

BELLE: *(Pause.)* What is your name?

YOUNG-SCROOGE: Mine?

BELLE: Yes.

(The carols end.)

YOUNG-SCROOGE: Ebenezer.

BELLE: Ebenezer?

YOUNG-SCROOGE: Ebenezer Scrooge.

BELLE: How quaint. *(SHE laughs.)*

YOUNG-SCROOGE: You find it humorous?

BELLE: It suits you.

YOUNG-SCROOGE: And yours?

BELLE: Belle.

YOUNG-SCROOGE: Belle…I shall never forget it.

BELLE: Well, perhaps I should join the others.

YOUNG-SCROOGE: Dance with me.

BELLE: There isn't music.

(From off we hear a slow tune.)

YOUNG-SCROOGE: There, you see, it was meant to be.

BELLE: You're incorrigible, Master Ebenezer Scrooge.

(BELLE & YOUNG-SCROOGE slowly dance, then exit.)

PAST: You were happy?

SCROOGE: Indeed.

PAST: It takes so little to raise the spirits of those around us.

SCROOGE: What a fool I've been?

PAST: Is something the matter?

SCROOGE: I should like to be able to say a word or two to my clark just now, that's all.

PAST: Is this remorse, I see?

SCROOGE: Nonsense.

PAST: You could bring happiness. To provide such memories and joy, it cost the Fezziwig's mere pounds of mortal money—

SCROOGE: If he had been wise he would have invested it in something else than an evening of drinking and games. Napoleon's war nearly bankrupted the country. Fezziwig was a fool; he lost everything and died a pauper.

PAST: …my time grows short—quick!

(Shift: To DICKENS at his desk.)

DICKENS: *(Repeats the line:)* "My time grows short," observed the Spirit. "Quick!" This was not addressed to Scrooge, or to any one whom he could see, but it produced an immediate effect. For again Scrooge saw himself. He was older now, a man in the prime of life. His face had not the harsh and rigid lines of later years; but it had begun to wear with the signs of care and avarice. There was an eager, greedy, restless motion in the eye, which showed the passion that had taken root, and where the shadow of the growing tree would fall.
(Shift: A London street, LADY-BELLE and ADULT-SCROOGE are revealed.)
He was not alone, but stood by the side of a fair young girl in mourning-dress: in whose eyes there were tears.

LADY-BELLE: Will you be coming to dinner?

ADULT-SCROOGE: Business calls. I have a foreclosure to attend.

LADY-BELLE: On Christmas Eve?

ADULT-SCROOGE: Finance waits for no man, you know that Belle.

LADY-BELLE: Of course. May I be cheeky and ask a question?

ADULT-SCROOGE: By all means.

LADY-BELLE: Mother and I were wondering when you intend to propose?

ADULT-SCROOGE: As soon as the matter of your dowry has been concluded.

LADY-BELLE: Ebenezer, my mother has no money for such an expense, you know that. I thought you loved me?

ADULT-SCROOGE: I do, but it would be imprudent to rush into such a bond. Has your mother made inquiries amongst the other relatives?

LADY-BELLE: Ebenezer, I do not wish to wait any longer, we're adults and I want children.

ADULT-SCROOGE: To produce children in our present financial condition would be irresponsible. I'm looking out for your interests.

LADY-BELLE: If you're not to marry me now—when?

ADULT-SCROOGE: When we are financially stable—

LADY-BELLE: You've been saying that for ten years.

ADULT-SCROOGE: Then stop asking. Forgive me, I do not mean to be glib. Belle, Belle, look at me. We're not like the others. Your brother ran into marriage and what's become of him? Dick lives in squalor with five screaming brats. I say we do this properly and wait until—

LADY-BELLE: I've grown weary of the situation—

ADULT-SCROOGE: And I've grown weary of the conversation!

LADY-BELLE: I never cared about money. I loved you…but apparently another idol has replaced me. *(Pause.)* I no longer believe you love me, Ebenezer.

ADULT-SCROOGE: Nonsense. You're prone to exaggeration, Belle.

LADY-BELLE: I have no just cause to grieve if it can cheer and comfort you in time to come, as I would have tried to do.

ADULT-SCROOGE: What Idol has displaced you?

LADY-BELLE: A golden one—

ADULT-SCROOGE: This is the evenhanded dealing of the world. There is nothing in the world so hard as poverty; and nothing poverty professes to condemn with such severity as the pursuit of wealth.

LADY-BELLE: You fear the world too much. All your other hopes have merged into the hope of being beyond the chance of its reproach. I have seen your nobler aspirations fall off one by one, until the master-passion, gain, engrosses you.

ADULT-SCROOGE: Even if what you say is true, I am not changed towards you.

LADY-BELLE: Ebenezer—

ADULT-SCROOGE: Stop it.

LADY-BELLE: Our contract is an old one. It was made when we were both poor and content to be so, until, in good season, we could improve our worldly fortune by our patient industry. You are changed. When it was made, you were another man.

ADULT-SCROOGE: I was a boy.

LADY-BELLE: How often and how keenly I have thought of this, I will not say. It is enough that I have thought of it. I think it best we part company?

ADULT-SCROOGE: Have I ever sought release?

LADY-BELLE: In words? No.

ADULT-SCROOGE: In what, then?

LADY-BELLE: In a changed nature and an altered spirit; in everything that made my love of any worth in your sight.

ADULT-SCROOGE: I didn't make this world, Belle; I am forced to succumb to its rules.

LADY-BELLE: We are at a crossroads, Ebenezer; you must choose the path your life will journey.

ADULT-SCROOGE: I do what I must faced with the responsibility of one day having a family.

LADY-BELLE: You speak of it as a burden. Tell me, if we never shared a past, would you seek me out, a dowerless girl and try to win me now? *(ADULT-SCROOGE looks away.)* I see. I release you, Ebenezer. With a full heart, for the love of him you once were. May you be happy in the life you have chosen.

> *(LADY-BELLE kisses ADULT-SCROOGE on the cheek and exits.)*

SCROOGE: Don't just stand there.

ADULT-SCROOGE: *(Half-heartedly.)* Belle?

SCROOGE: Go after her.

ADULT-SCROOGE: Humbug. *(HE exits.)*

SCROOGE: You fool! What are you doing? Belle? Belle! Beeeeeelle! Spirit, why do you delight to torture me?

PAST: Do not blame me. I told you these were shadows of the things that have been. They are of your past and your making.

SCROOGE: Remove me from this place. Do you hear? Haunt me no longer.

> *(Shift: Music, the ANGELS enter, dancing on point and surround SCROOGE. The light grows in a white-hot intensity and then plunge to black. DICKENS is revealed writing then reads his work.)*

DICKENS: "He was conscious of being exhausted, and overcome by an irresistible drowsiness; and, further, of being in his own bedroom. He gave his body; as if to reassure himself of being yet whole, a parting squeeze. Finding himself in one piece, Scrooge had barely time to reel to bed, before he sank into a heavy sleep. End of Stave Two." *(HE rises and calls.)* Darling? Catherine, come see what I've written. Catherine, are you there? Children? They've gone—they've gone and left me. *(HE sits. There is a knock at the door.)* Catherine? Is someone there?

PRIMM: *(Enters.)* Mr. Dickens, I hope you will forgive the intrusion.

DICKENS: This is most irregular. How did you get in?

PRIMM: My name is Primm, my card. I admitted myself of my own accord; took a bit of a wander accessing the place. *(Holds up a key.)*

DICKENS: Where did you get a key, Primm?

PRIMM: I represent the Bank of England; they own the deed to the property—

DICKENS: Get out!

PRIMM: Sir—

DICKENS: Get out, you have no right to be here.

PRIMM: Oh, but I do so, sir. The mortgage you've ignored is in arrears and foreclosure appears inevitable.

DICKENS: Until then, this is my property, get out—wait! How did you know I would be here?

PRIMM: Its Christmas time sir, most men are assured to be home with their families.

DICKENS: *(Rises.)* Be gone. Do you hear? Get out of my house! Now!

PRIMM: Very well, but you've not seen the last of me; next time I bring the Constable. I'll show myself out Mr. Dickens. This time of year—'tis a shame to be spending it alone.

>*(PRIMM exits. DICKENS sits, gulps a drink and then cradles his head in his hands. The lights fade.)*

INTERMISSION

CHARLES DICKENS PRESENTS
A CHRISTMAS CAROL

ACT II

In the darkness we hear another mournful tune, eventually the BEGGAR CHILD is revealed singing. CHARLES DICKENS is at his desk. The light cocoons him as if it is the writer's circle of attention. The hour chimes; it is a half hour later. DICKENS appearance is more disheveled. The CHILD exits with the completion of the song. DICKENS writes, pauses, then reads.

DICKENS: Awaking in the middle of a prodigiously tough snore, and sitting up in bed to get his thoughts together, Scrooge felt that he was restored to consciousness in the right nick of time, for the especial purpose of holding a conference with the second messenger dispatched by Jacob Marley. Now, being prepared for almost anything, he was not by any means prepared for nothing; and, consequently, when the Bell struck one, he was taken with a violent fit of trembling.

>   *(Shift: A bell tolls one. Music, CHRISTMAS PRESENT and SCROOGE are revealed in Scrooge's bedroom.)*

PRESENT: Come forth. Come forth and know me better, man!

SCROOGE: Who are you?

PRESENT: I am the Ghost of Christmas Present!

SCROOGE: Look at this magnificence.

PRESENT: You have never seen the like of me before!

SCROOGE: Never!

PRESENT: Have you never walked with the younger members of my family?

SCROOGE: I am afraid I have not.

PRESENT: Yet you might have had you chosen to leave this place and walk forth with my brothers.

SCROOGE: Have you many, Spirit?

PRESENT: More than eighteen hundred.

SCROOGE: A tremendous family to provide for.

PRESENT: Are you ready to walk amongst your fellow men?

SCROOGE: Have I a choice?

PRESENT: In life there is always a choice, Ebenezer.

SCROOGE: Spirit, conduct me where you will.

PRESENT: Touch my robe!

SCROOGE: Where will you take me?

PRESENT: The streets of Camden Town. It is Christmas day, Ebenezer.

(Shift: To DICKENS at his desk)

DICKENS: Scrooge did as he was told, and held fast. All vanished instantly and they stood in the city streets on Christmas morning.
> *(Shift: Music, the street fills with Carolers singing. They transform the street into the CRATCHIT home.)*

The shop windows were laden with an array of meals yet to come. The windows were stuffed full of holly, mistletoe, red berries, ivy, turkeys, geese, game, poultry, brawn, meat, pigs, sausages, oysters, pies, puddings, fruit and punch. Perhaps it was the Spirit's own generous nature and sympathy for all poor men that led him straight to the threshold of the home of Scrooge's Clark, Bob Cratchit. *(PETER, JACK and MRS. CRATCHIT are revealed.)* The Spirit smiled and paused to bless the four-roomed house.

(DICKENS exits.)

SCROOGE: What place is this?

PRESENT: The home of your clark, Bob Cratchit.

MRS CRATCHIT: Peter Cratchit, hurry up and help your sister.

PETER: I can't get this collar to close.

MRS CRATCHIT: Breathe in, hold it and then fasten it.

PETER: *(Takes a mighty breath.)* Ah-hup.

JACK: You should make your cravat look like mine. Mine is correct. I've even tied an Osbaldiston knot.

PETER: Go away.

JACK: Mother, Peter isn't really trying to fix his cravat properly. My collar and tie are very straight. I've even tied it in a proper Osbaldiston knot, worn by all the gentlemen. Don't I look smart mother?

MRS CRATCHIT: Yes, Jack, you look magnificent.
JACK: Thank you, mother.

GILLIAN & MIRANDA *(Enter.)*: The goose! The goose! We smell the goose!

PETER: I can't get this thing to work.

GILLIAN: What's the matter?

PETER: My collar.

MIRANDA: Why don't you fasten it?

PETER: I'm trying.

GILLIAN: Mother, when is Martha to come home, she's been gone for months?

MRS CRATCHIT: Her work requires she always be present to serve. I expect her at any moment.

GILLIAN: Can we have a piece of the goose?

MRS CRATCHIT: Not until dinner.

MIRANDA: We're hungry.

JACK: Mother, they're trying to steal a piece of the goose.

MRS CRATCHIT: When your father comes we'll eat—not before.

PETER: I've mastered the cravat!

> *(PETER has blindfolded himself with the tie. ALL laugh.)*

MRS CRATCHIT: Belinda, give him a hand.

BELINDA: *(Enters.)* Yes, mother.

MIRANDA: Peter looks funny.

GILLIAN & MIRANDA: Peter looks silly! Silly goose!

PETER: I look like a gentleman.

BELINDA: You have to hold still. *(BELINDA wraps PETER on the head with her knuckles.)*

PETER: Ow!

MRS CRATCHIT: Whatever has got your precious sister Martha? She wasn't as late coming last Christmas Day by half an hour.

MARTHA: *(Pops in surprising ALL.)* No worries, I'm here now.

CHILDREN: It's Martha, mother. Merry Christmas! Hello Martha!

MARTHA: I want a hug! *(SHE hugs all the children.)*

MRS CRATCHIT: Children, run along. Why, bless your heart alive, my dear, how late you are.

MARTHA: We'd a deal of work to finish up last night and had to clear table this morning.

MRS CRATCHIT: A girl your age shouldn't have to go to work.

MARTHA: I don't mind, mother.

MRS CRATCHIT: I worry about you living there. You're thin and you eyes have dark circles under them.

MARTHA: I'm fine.

MRS CRATCHIT: Do they have a nurse?

MARTHA: All the women look after one another.

MRS CRATCHIT: It's not right, a young girl working fourteen and fifteen hours a day, seven days a week.

MARTHA: I manage.

MRS CRATCHIT: That's not what we wanted for you.

MARTHA: I've saved a bit of extra money. *(SHE hands it to her mother.)*

MRS CRATCHIT: You keep it.

MARTHA: I meant it for the family.

MRS CRATCHIT: *(THEY hug.)* I love you, my duck.

PETER: *(Hiding.)* Are you ready to see a gent about town? *(He dramatically reveals himself. The other children tumble in after him. HE strikes a pose. The cravat is tied in a bow in his hair.)* Look one, look all!

MARTHA: Peter, you goose.

PETER: *(Campy:)* I am a fair maiden.

JACK: I told Peter that was not the proper way to wear a cravat. My cravat is the proper way to wear one. I've even tied it an Osbaldiston knot like all the London swells.

MRS CRATCHIT: Peter, I'll make you wear it in your hair to church if you don't put it on properly this minute. Martha, sit you down, my dear, and have a warm, Lord bless you.

BELINDA: *(CRATCHIT is heard singing.)* Father's coming, hide everyone. Hide, Martha, hide!

PETER: I'm hiding here.

> *(PETER stands in the middle of the room and throws a blanket over his head. The other CHILDREN noisily hide under the table.)*

ALL: Sh!!!

> *(Enter CRATCHIT & TINY TIM.)*

CRATCHIT: Merry Christmas everyone.

MRS CRATCHIT: And a Merry Christmas to you, Bob. How are we, my precious Tim?

TIM: I heard the carolers at St. Paul's.

MRS CRATCHIT: You did?

TIM: It was most lovely.

CRATCHIT: Where are all the children?

MRS CRATCHIT: Peter is standing there in the middle of the room.

PETER: *(From under the blanket.)* I am not.

JACK: I told him not to hide there.

ALL CHILDREN: Sh!

CRATCHIT: Where are the rest of the children?

MRS CRATCHIT: Not coming.

CRATCHIT: What about Martha?

MRS CRATCHIT: Not coming.

CRATCHIT: And Belinda?

MRS CRATCHIT: Not coming.

CRATCHIT: And Gillian?

MRS CRATCHIT: Not coming.

CRATCHIT: Miranda?

MRS CRATCHIT: Not coming.

CRATCHIT: And Jack?

MRS CRATCHIT: Not coming. Not a one.

CRATCHIT: On Christmas day?

ALL CHILDREN: *(Emerging.)* Here we are father! *(They hug CRATCHIT.)*

MRS CRATCHIT: All of you take Tim and play. *(The CHILDREN exit.)* And how did little Tim behave?

CRATCHIT: As good as gold, and better. Somehow he gets thoughtful, sitting by himself so much, and thinks the strangest things you ever heard.

MRS CRATCHIT: What did he say, Bob?

CRATCHIT: He told me, coming home, that he hoped the people saw him in the church, because he was a cripple and it might be pleasant for them to remember upon Christmas Day, who made lame beggars walk and blind men see.

MRS CRATCHIT: Oh, Bob.

(CRATCHIT and MRS CRATCHIT embrace.)

SCROOGE: Spirit, will the boy do without his crutch one day?

PRESENT: His spirit is strong, but he has a terrible sickness.

SCROOGE: Is there no cure?

PRESENT: Yes, but not for the poor.

MRS CRATCHIT: Children, time to eat.

(ALL gather around the table.)

BELINDA: I helped with dinner.

JACK: I tried to keep Peter out of trouble while Mother prepared the meal.

MIRANDA: I helped with the bread.

GILLIAN: I helped with the pudding.

CRATCHIT: And what did you do, Peter?

PETER: I licked the spoon.

CRATCHIT: What is that smell?

MIRANDA: It's the goose.

(MRS CRATCHIT presents the goose. ALL applaud.)

CRATCHIT: Children, your mother has out done herself this year. God bless us.

TIM: God bless us everyone.

CRATCHIT: Indeed, Tim, indeed. Let us give thanks.

(The CRATCHIT'S bow their head in prayer.)

SCROOGE: It is such a little goose for so many.

PRESENT: They shall not find it so. Tonight they feast

upon the love of their family and groan under the weight like fatted kings.

SCROOGE: Spirit, tell me if Tiny Tim will live.

PRESENT: *(Pause.)* I see a vacant chair, in the poor chimney corner and a crutch without an owner, carefully preserved. If these shadows remain unaltered by the future, the child will die.

SCROOGE: No, no, kind Spirit, say he will be spared.

PRESENT: If these shadows remain unaltered, none other of my race will find him here. What then? If he be like to die, he had better do it, and decrease the surplus population.

(CRATCHIT ends the prayer.)

CRATCHIT: Children, let us raise a glass. I give you Mr. Scrooge, the founder of the feast.

MRS CRATCHIT: The founder of the feast—indeed. I wish I had him here, I'd give him a piece of my mind to feast upon and I hope he'd have a good appetite for it.

CRATCHIT: My dear, the children, its Christmas Day?

MRS CRATCHIT: It should be Christmas Day, I am sure, on which one drinks the health of such an odious, stingy, hard, unfeeling man as Mr. Scrooge.

CRATCHIT: Darling—

MRS CRATCHIT: You know he is, Robert. Nobody knows it better than you, poor fellow.

CRATCHIT: It's Christmas Day.

MRS CRATCHIT: I'll drink his health for your sake and the Day's, not for his. Long life to him. A merry Christmas and a happy New Year. He'll be very merry and very happy I have no doubt!

TIM: Mr. Scrooge.

ALL: *(Reluctantly.)* Mr. Scrooge.

CRATCHIT: Now then, a song.

>*(ALL clap and cheer as CRATCHIT starts singing. The family joins in.)*

PRESENT: Touch my robe. *(HE grabs PRESENTS' robe.)* We have many stops Ebenezer.

>*(Shift: DICKENS is at work.)*

DICKENS: He did as the Spirit commanded. The Ghost left the city and together they sped above the black and heaving sea. It was a great surprise to Scrooge, while listening to the moaning of the wind and thinking what a solemn thing it was to traverse the lonely darkness over the unknown abyss of ocean, whose depths were as secret and profound as Death—it was a great surprise to Scrooge, to hear a hearty laugh.
>*(Shift: FRED, TOPPER, GWENDOLYN, and MS. GUMMAGE are revealed. FRED'S group picks up the song the CRATCHITS were singing.)*

It was a much greater surprise to Scrooge to recognize it as his own nephew's. It was an even greater surprise to find himself in a bright, dry, gleaming room, with the Spirit standing by his side and smiling at his nephew with approving affability.

> *(DICKENS exits. TOPPER sings the final stanza in a very hammy manner. At the end of the song, FRED and his guests burst into laughter and applause.)*

FRED: Well done, Topper old man. You're in fine voice this evening.

TOPPER: *(Bowing.)* Thank you one and all.

FRED: I had never had the courage for amateur theatricals. It should prove quite sporting.

TOPPER: It is my passion, Fred, to play upon the stage.

FRED: Has your company of actors picked a title?

TOPPER: The great Shakespearean tragedy of passion and conquest: Antony & Cleopatra. I shall don the role of the soldier and lover, Marc Antony. We are in need of a Cleopatra. Perhaps Ms. Gummage, you desire to tread the boards? You know, I will be casting the production; I could put in a word on your behalf.

MS. GUMMAGE: Thank you all the same Mr. Topper, but I dread the ferocity of your Antony would put my humble talents to shame.

TOPPER: Nonsense, Ms. Gummage, I would be awed in your presence as I am now.

> *(THEY laugh and MS. GUMMAGE moves further away from TOPPER.)*

MS. GUMMAGE: Shame upon you, Mr. Topper.

TOPPER: What we really need is money. It is tragic that we artists are forced to compromise our vision to economic constraints. We fall from the poetry of art to the prose of mundane life.

GWENDOLYN: Fred, would your Uncle Scrooge back the players?

FRED: Not by half. My darling Gwendolyn, the holiday season has blackened his mood.

TOPPER: Surely, you jest.

FRED: As I live, he said that Christmas was a humbug and he believed it too!

GWENDOLYN: More shame for him, Fred.

FRED: Oh, darling, he's a comical old fellow that's the truth: and not so pleasant as he might be. However, his offences carry their own punishment and I have nothing to say against him.

TOPPER: I'm sure he is very rich, Fred, at least you always report so.

FRED: What of that? His wealth is of no use to him. He does no good with it.

GWENDOLYN: I have no patience for the man.

FRED: Oh, I have. I am sorry for him; I couldn't be angry with him if I tried. Who suffers by his ill will? Himself always. Here, he takes it into his head to dislike us and refuses to come and dine. What's the consequence? He misses an exquisite dinner.

MS. GUMMAGE: Indeed, I think he missed a very good dinner.

TOPPER: Well said, Ms. Gummage.

FRED: What do you say, Topper?

TOPPER: I know the sadness of his life, for I too, am a bachelor. Condemned to live alone, eat alone; sip my port alone—if only I could find the right women. For it is the fairer sex that is the compass charting a man's ship to happiness…wouldn't you agree Ms. Gummage?

MS. GUMMAGE: If you follow the course you've currently set upon you never shall find harbor in my port.

(ALL laugh.)

TOPPER: Dashed upon the rocks, again.

MS. GUMMAGE: You are such a ridiculous fellow.

TOPPER: And you—a beautiful mermaid.

GWENDOLYN: Where were we, Fred?

FRED: I was only going to say, that the consequence of his taking a dislike to us and not making merry—he loses some very pleasant moments, which could do him no harm. I mean to give him the same chance every year, whether he likes it or not. He may rail at Christmas till he dies, but he can't help thinking better of it. I defy him, if he finds me going there, in good temper, year after year and saying,

"Uncle Scrooge, how are you?" I think I shook him yesterday.

GWENDOLYN: Hardly.

FRED: I tell you it's true.

TOPPER: If I had Mr. Scrooge's money, I would shower it all upon you, Ms. Gummage. You would be London's Cleopatra and I, your Hyde Park Antony. Oh fair Queen of the Nile, Rome is yours for the asking, bid Antony do anything and it shall be done.

MS. GUMMAGE: Get off my barge.

TOPPER: "I am dying, Egypt, dying."

GWENDOLYN: I believe, Ms. Gummage has rung the curtain down upon you, Mr. Topper.

MS. GUMMAGE: With no call for an encore.

TOPPER: Cut to the quick.

> *(TOPPER dies a mock death. ALL laugh and applaud.)*

FRED: What do you say to playing a game?

SCROOGE: I love games!

TOPPER: *(Bolting up.)* Blind man's buff!

FRED: I have a new one.

GWENDOLYN: Do tell us, Fred.

FRED: It's called 'yes and no'.

TOPPER: Have you the rules?

FRED: It's quite simple. I think of something and you have to find out what it is by asking me questions. I answer 'yes or no' as the case requires. Are we for it?

TOPPER: It sounds delicious, count me in.

GWENDOLYN: I as well.

MS. GUMMAGE: I make a fourth.

SCROOGE: I shall win, my boy!

PRESENT: Ebenezer it is time we go.

SCROOGE: Not now, Spirit. Here is a new game. One half hour, Spirit, please?

PRESENT: As you wish.

SCROOGE: Let's to it, Fred.

FRED: Give me a tick. Ah! I've got it.

TOPPER: Are you thinking of a mineral?

FRED: No.

GWENDOLYN: An animal?

FRED: Yes.

MS. GUMMAGE: A live animal?

FRED: Yes.

TOPPER: Is it a rather disagreeable animal?

FRED: Yes.

SCROOGE: A nasty animal is it?

GWENDOLYN: Is it savage?

FRED: Yes!

MS. GUMMAGE: An animal that growls and grunts?

FRED: In a manner of speaking, yes.

TOPPER: Is it a tiger?

FRED: No.

SCROOGE: Let me have a turn.

GWENDOLYN: Is it killed at market?

FRED: No.

MS. GUMMAGE: Is it a horse?

FRED: No.

TOPPER: An ass?

FRED: *(Smiling.)* Not in a literal sense.

SCROOGE: I am absolutely stumped. Wait—is it a cow?

GWENDOLYN: What about a cow?

FRED: No.

MS. GUMMAGE: Bull?

FRED: No.

TOPPER: Bear?

FRED: Yes and no.

SCROOGE: Yes and no?

GWENDOLYN: Is it a Dog?

FRED: No.

MS. GUMMAGE: Pig?

FRED: No.

TOPPER: Does it live in London and walk about the streets?

FRED: Yes.

SCROOGE: A pet of some kind, aye?

GWENDOLYN: A cat?

FRED: No.

MS. GUMMAGE: E-gads! I figure it out…it's a rutabaga!

ALL: A rutabaga?

MS. GUMMAGE: It was a guess.

TOPPER: I think I have it! I know what it is, Fred, I'm certain.

FRED: What?

SCROOGE: For God sakes, man, spill it already. What?

TOPPER: It's your Uncle Scro-o-o-oge!

(ALL laugh. FRED raises his glass.)

FRED: He has given us plenty of merriment, and it would be ungrateful not to drink his health. I say, A Merry Christmas and a Happy New Year to the old man, whatever he is. He wouldn't take it from me, but may he have it—Uncle Scrooge.

ALL: *(Toasting.)* Uncle Scrooge!

SCROOGE: Hum…bug.

TOPPER: Ms. Gummage have I mentioned how lovely you look this evening?

MS GUMMAGE: You could tell me over a glass of champagne.

FRED: Let us retire to the parlor. Ladies, after you. Topper, give us a song old boy.

(TOPPER begins and ALL join in.)

SCROOGE: Hum…bug.

PRESENT: We must go, Ebenezer.

(Shift: DICKENS is revealed.)

DICKENS: It was a long night, if it were only a night; but Scrooge had his doubts of this, because the Christmas holidays appeared to be condensed into the space of time they passed together. It was strange, too, that while Scrooge remained unaltered in his outward form, the Ghost grew older, clearly older. Scrooge had observed this change, but never spoke of it until they stood together in an open place.

(DICKENS exits. Shift: A roadside. PRESENT looks haggard. Thunder ensues.)

SCROOGE: Spirit, what has happened? You look pale and worn.

PRESENT: My life upon this globe, is very brief.

SCROOGE: Are spirits' lives so short?

PRESENT: It ends to night.

SCROOGE: Tonight?

(A bell tolls.)

PRESENT: Tonight at midnight. Hark! The time is drawing near.

(PRESENT'S robe begins to undulate and snarling is heard. PRESENT looks to his feet. Suddenly a claw-like hand shoots out from beneath HIS robe. SCROOGE recoils in fright.)

SCROOGE: Lord bless me. Spirit, what is it?

PRESENT: Look, look here, what man has wrought.

SCROOGE: No, spirit.

PRESENT: Behold, Ebenezer Scrooge.

> *(PRESENT draws forth IGNORANCE and WANT from beneath his robes. SCROOGE gasps as the children suckle from PRESENT'S body.)*

SCROOGE: Spirit, are they yours?

PRESENT: They are Man's, and they cling to me, appealing from their fathers. This boy is Ignorance. This girl is Want. Beware them both, and all of their kind, but most of all beware the boy, for on his brow I see written that which is doom, unless the writing be erased.

SCROOGE: Have they no refuge or resource?

PRESENT: Are there no prisons? *(A bell tolls.)* Are there no workhouses? *(The bell tolls again.)*

SCROOGE: Spirit—

> *(The bell begins a count to twelve as the stage fills with fog.)*

PRESENT: Man, if man you be in heart, forbear that wicked cant until you have discovered what the surplus is, and where it is. *(The bell tolls.)* Will you decide what men shall live and what men shall die? *(The bell tolls.)* It may be, that in the sight of Heaven, you are more worthless and less fit to live than millions like these poor children. *(The *bell tolls.)* Oh God! To hear the insect on the leaf pronouncing on the too much life among his hungry brothers in the dust!

SCROOGE: *(The bell tolls.)* Do not leave me, Spirit. Have mercy.

PRESENT: Mercy. MERCY? I HAVE NONE TO GIVE!

> *(An explosion of thunder with all the force of the heavens is unleashed. PRESENT disappears into the fog. Shift: DICKENS is within his circle. He reads.)*

DICKENS: As the bell struck twelve, Scrooge looked about him for the ghost and saw it not. As the last stroke ceased to vibrate he remembered the predication of old Jacob Marley and lifting up his eyes, beheld a solemn Phantom, draped and hooded, shrouded in a black garment, coming, like a mist towards him. He felt that it was tall and stately and that its mysterious presence filled him with a solemn dread.

> *(Shift: There is a final overwhelming toll of the bell shifting to a single sustained note. FUTURE & SCROOGE are revealed in a sea of endless black and fog.)*

SCROOGE: Am I in the presence of the Ghost of Christmas Yet To Come? *(No response.)* You are about to show me shadows of the things that have not happened, but will happen in the time before us, is that so, Spirit? *(No response.)* Ghost of the Future…I fear you more than any spectre I have seen. But as I know your purpose is to do me good and as I hope to live to be another man from what I was, I am prepared to bear you company and do it with a thankful heart. Will you not speak to me? *(No response.)* The night is waning fast, and it is precious to me. Lead on, Spirit.

(Shift: FUTURE points, thunder ensues and CHINFOLD, SPRY, and SNUFF are revealed on a street.)

MR CHINFOLD: No, I don't know much about it, either way. I only know he's dead.

MRS SNUFF: I thought he'd never die!

MR SPRY: When did it happen?

MR CHINFOLD: Last night, I believe.

MRS SNUFF: Why, what was the matter with him?

MR CHINFOLD: God knows. I imagine a cold heart.

MRS SPRY: What's he done with his money?

MR CHINFOLD: I haven't heard, left it to his Company, perhaps. All I know is he hasn't left it to me.

(ALL laugh.)

MRS SNUFF: It's likely to be a very cheap funeral, for upon my life I don't know anybody going.

MR SPRY: That's the way he would have wanted it, a cut-rate affair.

MRS SNUFF: Suppose we make up a party and volunteer?

MR CHINFOLD: I don't mind going if a lunch is provided, but I must be fed.

(ALL laugh.)

MR SPRY: Well, I am the most disinterested among you, but I'll offer to go, if anybody else will. When I come to think of it, I'm not at all sure that I wasn't his most particular friend; for once he stopped me in the street to demand the time.

(ALL laugh and exit.)

SCROOGE: If there is any person in the town, who feels emotion caused by this man's death? Show that person to me, Spirit, I beseech you.

(Shift: FUTURE points, thunder ensues. In an alley, JOE, LAUNDRESS, the UNDERTAKER and the CHARWOMEN are revealed.)

CHARWOMEN: Out of my way. I ought to have first crack at selling my items to Joe, that I should. He should see my used goods first, aye Joe?

UNDERTAKER: It was I brung you in the first place.

JOE: Now-now-now. Let the laundress alone to be the first. Let the undertaker's man alone to be the second; and let the charwomen alone to be the third. Come here deary, what odds have you there?

LAUNDRESS: I don't feel bad for taking his goods. Every person has a right to take care of themselves, he always did.

CHARWOMEN: That's true, indeed, no man more so.

JOE: Why then, don't stand staring as if you was afraid, woman; who's the wiser?

LAUNDRESS: I say, who's the worse for the loss of a few things like these? Not a dead man, I suppose.

CHARWOMEN: No, indeed.

LAUNDRESS: If he wanted to keep 'em after he was dead, the wicked old screw, why wasn't he more natural in his lifetime? If he had been, he'd have had somebody to look after him when he was struck with Death, instead of lying gasping out his last there, alone by himself.

CHARWOMEN: It's the truest word that ever was spoke, it's a judgment on him.

JOE: Open the bundle and let me know the value of it. Speak out plain. It's no sin.

LAUNDRESS: Sheets, towels, two old-fashioned silver teaspoons, a pair of sugar-tongs and a boot.

JOE: *(Scribbles on a slate.)* There's your account. No back talk. I always give too much to the ladies. A weakness of mine, they'll be the ruin of me. Oo is next?

UNDERTAKER: I am.

JOE: Then get on with it, before I wither myself. Come on, what you got?

UNDERTAKER: A seal, a pencil-case, a pair of sleeve-buttons and a brooch.

JOE: *(Adds the figures.)* There's your account and I

wouldn't give another sixpence, if I was to be boiled for it.

CHARWOMEN: And now undo my bundle, Joe.

JOE: What do you call this? Bed-curtains. You don't mean to say you took 'em down, rings and all, with him lying there?

CHARWOMEN: Yes I do. Why not?

JOE: *(Laughs.)* You were born to make your fortune.

CHARWOMEN: *(Wipes his nose.)* Don't smear upon his blanket, now.

JOE: *His* blanket? *(Drops it.)*

CHARWOMEN: Who's else's do you think? He isn't likely to take cold without 'em, I dare say.

JOE: I hope he didn't die of nothing catching? Eh?

CHARWOMEN: Don't you be afraid of that, I ain't so fond of his company that I'd loiter about for such things, if he did. *(JOE closely scans the cloth.)* Ah! You may look through that shirt till your eye ache; but you won't find a hole in it. It's the best he had. They'd have wasted it, if it hadn't been for me.

JOE: What do you call wasting of it?

CHARWOMEN: Putting it on him to be buried. Somebody was fool enough to do it, but I took it off him again.

JOE: Right off the body?

CHARWOMEN: Well he won't dress for a Last Supper where he's bound.

JOE: Right then, let's settle up in the parlor.

(ALL laugh and exit.)

SCROOGE: Spirit. I see, I see. The case of this unhappy man might be my own. My life tends that way, now. Please spirit, show me some compassion in death.

(Shift: FUTURE points, thunder ensues and The CHILDREN, CRATCHIT and MRS CRATCHIT are revealed in a debtors grave yard standing near a tiny body wrapped in broadcloth with TINY TIM'S crutch lain upon it.)

CRATCHIT: *(Reads.)* "Seeing the crowds, he went up on the mountains, and when he sat down his disciples came to him. And he opened his mouth and taught them saying: Blessed are the poor in spirit, for theirs is the kingdom of heaven. Blessed are those who mourn, for they shall be comforted. Blessed are the meek for they shall inherit the earth. Blessed are those who hunger and thirst for righteousness, for they shall be satisfied. Blessed are the merciful, for they shall obtain mercy. Blessed are the pure in heart, for they shall see God…" *(CRATCHIT cannot continue.)*

SCROOGE: *(Quietly)* No, spirit, tell me the boy did not die. Please, spirit. I can't bare it.

(Shift: FUTURE points, thunder ensues and SCROOGE stands before a huge gravestone.)

SCROOGE: Spirit. This is a fearful place. Why have you

brought me to the Spittle field graveyard? I do not wish to be here.

(FUTURE points to the gravestone. SCROOGE starts toward it and stops.)

SCROOGE: I understand you and I would do it, if I could. But I have not the power, Spirit. I have not the power. Answer me one question. Are these the shadows of the things that will be or are they shadows of things that may be?

(FUTURE points again. Thunder and fog builds.)

SCROOGE: Men's courses will foreshadow certain ends, to which, if persevered in, they must lead, but if the courses be departed from, the ends will change. Say it is thus with what you show me.

(FUTURE vigorously points. SCROOGE approaches the head stone. There is a flash of lightening and his name is revealed upon the stone.)

SCROOGE: No, Spirit. Oh no, no!

(Thunder and lightning grows as FUTURE sinks into Scrooge's grave.)

SCROOGE: Spirit, hear me! I am not the man I was. I will not be the man I must have been but for this intercourse. Why show me this, if I am past all hope? Spirit? Spirit?

(Shift: DICKENS is revealed.)

DICKENS: In his agony, he clawed to grasp the spectral figure's robe, the spirit being stronger, repulsed him.

Holding up his hands in a last prayer to have his fate reversed, he cried, "Oh, tell me I may sponge away the writing on the stone," but the Phantom had disappeared.
> *(Shift: Light slowly fills the room. SCROOGE is revealed in his bed.)*

Morning permeated the room, Scrooge hardly noticed for he had been sobbing so violently in his conflict with the Spirit, that his face was wet with tears. *(DICKENS exits.)*

SCROOGE: *(Tossing in his bed.)* I will not shut out the lessons, I will honor Christmas in my heart, I will keep it all the year, I will not…*(HE awakens.)* Where am I? My room. My bedchamber. I'm alive. I'm alive! I can't believe it. The spirits did it. They did it all in one night! I must get dressed. *(HE begins to dress.)* I don't know what to do? I am as light as a feather, I am as happy as an angel; I am as merry as a schoolboy. I am as giddy as a drunken man. A merry Christmas to everyone! A happy New Year to the entire world! Hallo, happy New Year bed! Whoop! Hallo, Merry Christmas there, old wardrobe! I don't know what day of the month it is! I don't know how long I've been among the Spirits. I don't know anything. I'm quite a baby. Never mind. I don't care. I'd rather be a baby. Hallo! Whoop! I feel like laughing! I know, I shall give it a try.

> *(SCROOGE tries with all his might but only exhales air. He regroups and tries again this time a single note is emitted.)*

SCROOGE: Aaaaa—ha. I did it! I did it! I laughed. HA!

> *(SCROOGE, now dressed, clicks his heels together then kneels and speaks solemnly.)*

SCROOGE: Jacob Marley…thank you. I will live in the Past, the Present, and the Future. The Spirits of all Three shall strive within me. Oh Jacob Marley, Heaven and the Christmas Time be praised for this! I promise it, old Jacob; I promise it. I must be on my way.

(Shift: SCROOGE exits. The ENSEMBLE AND DOYCE enter singing on a London street.)

SCROOGE: *(Enters.)* Oh, glorious. Glorious. You there, boy. Come here, I won't hurt you. *(DOYCE timidly approaches.)* That's a lad. Tell me, what is today?

DOYCE: What's that?

SCROOGE: What's today—what day is it my fine fellow?

DOYCE: Today? Why, it's Christmas Day.

SCROOGE: Christmas Day? I haven't missed it. The Spirits have done it all in one night. They can do anything they like. Of course they can, they're spirits! My fine fellow?

DOYCE: My mum says I shouldn't talk to strangers, especially old ones a bit daft in the head.

SCROOGE: Your mother is right, but I've never felt saner. What is your name, young man?

DOYCE: Daniel Doyce and it please you sir.

SCROOGE: Doyce, that's an Irish name?

DOYCE: That it is sir, upon my father's side.

SCROOGE: How delightful. Tell me, young Master Doyce, do you know the Poulterer's, in the next street the one, at the corner?

DOYCE: I should hope I did.

SCROOGE: An intelligent boy—a remarkable boy. Do you know whether they've sold the prize Turkey in the window?

DOYCE: What, the one as big as me?

SCROOGE: What a delightful boy, its a pleasure to talk to you. Yes, Master Daniel Doyce, the one as big as you.

DOYCE: It's hanging there now.
SCROOGE: Is it? Go and buy it.

DOYCE: Go on, you can't be serious!

SCROOGE: No, no, I am in earnest. Go and buy it, and tell 'em to bring it here, that I may give them the direction where to take it. Come back with the man and I'll give you a shilling. Come back with him in less than five minutes and I'll give you half-a-crown.

DOYCE: For that I'd carry it here me-self.

SCROOGE: Run, Master Doyce, run!

(DOYCE races off as the TOWN PERSON enters.)

TOWN PERSON: Good day, sir.

(SCROOGE grabs them.)

SCROOGE: I'll send the turkey to Bob Cratchits!

TOWN PERSON: What's that?

SCROOGE: He shan't know who sent it

TOWN PERSON: I have no idea what you're on about.

SCROOGE: It's twice the size of Tiny Tim.

TOWN PERSON: Good. May I go now?

SCROOGE: Of course, and Merry Christmas to you.

TOWN PERSON: Merry Christmas.

>(The TOWN PERSON races off. SCROOGE spies the PHILANTHROPISTS.)

PHIL 2: *(Ringing a bell.)* We seek donations for the poor and destitute. Give what you can for the less fortunate.

SCROOGE: My dear sir, a merry Christmas to you!

PHIL 1: Ugh! It's Mr. Head.

PHIL 2: His name is Scrooge.

SCROOGE: Yes, that is my name, and I fear it may not be pleasant to you.

PHIL 2: I reserve judgement given the season.

SCROOGE: Allow me to ask your pardon. And will you have the goodness to accept—here, put me down for...

>(SCROOGE writes in the ledger. PHIL 2's eyes grow round.)

PHIL 2: Lord bless me! My dear Mr. Scrooge, are you

serious?

PHIL 1: Is he still having a problem with the bed?

PHIL 2: He's donating...

> *(PHIL 2 points inside the ledger. PHIL 1 turns to SCROOGE)*

PHIL 1: *(Quietly.)* Mr. Head, thank you.

> *(PHIL 1 plants a kiss right on SCROOGE'S lips.)*

PHIL 2: He can't help himself.

SCROOGE: Either can I. And a great many back payments are included in it, I assure you.

PHIL 2: My dear sir, we don't know what to say to such munificence—

SCROOGE: Say nothing. Please, come and see me. Will you come and see me?

PHIL 1: We will Mr. Head, we will!

PHIL 2: Merry Christmas, Mr. Scrooge.

> *(SCROOGE turns and collides with GWENDOLYN.)*

GWENDOLYN: You've knocked my packages to the ground.

SCROOGE: Please forgive me. Let me help you.

GWENDOLYN: It's quite all right.

SCROOGE: Bless me, I know you. You're my nephew's wife.

GWENDOLYN: Pardon?

SCROOGE: Gwendolyn is it?

GWENDOLYN: Yes.

SCROOGE: I am Fred's Uncle, Ebenezer Scrooge.

GWENDOLYN: I have heard so much about you.

(GWENDOLYN starts to turn away.)

SCROOGE: Do not be afraid. I have so many regrets. I beg you, forgive a foolish old man. I would give anything to make your acquaintance. Is it possible to start anew?

GWENDOLYN: Well, I don't know what to say…of course it is, Uncle.

(GWENDOLYN hugs SCROOGE. FRED approaches.)

FRED: Is everything all right, my love?

SCROOGE: Fred?

FRED: Why bless my soul.

SCROOGE: 'Tis I, your Uncle Scrooge. I wish to come to dinner. Will you let me, Fred?

FRED: Let you? Have a mercy, of course, Uncle.

SCROOGE: Thank you, nephew, thank you. Shall I bring anything?

FRED: A healthy appetite. We dine at half past three—oh, and Uncle?

SCROOGE: Yes?

FRED: Do you like games?

SCROOGE: I love games!

FRED: You'll be delighted to know that I've discovered a new one.

SCROOGE: What do you call it?

FRED: Yes and No!

SCROOGE: Fred, I will play any game in the world but 'Yes and No.' How about a good old fashioned round of Blind Man's Buff?

FRED: That we shall, Uncle.

GWENDOLYN: Merry Christmas, Uncle Ebenezer.

SCROOGE: And a Merry Christmas to you.

> *(Carolers begin a tune as THEY exit. Shift: DICKENS is revealed as CATHERINE and the CHILDREN come pouring in. DICKENS runs to his wife and embraces her. The tune fades.)*

KATE: Papa, papa, we're back!

WALTER: Quack!

BOZ: Can we sing carols now?

DICKENS: Of course we can. Catherine, forgive me? I've been a dull heartless buffoon.

CATHERINE: I don't care about the house or the money, I want only you.

MARY: Daddy, I prayed real hard and now my doll's numbly nose is better.

DICKENS: It is?

WALTER: Quack.

MARY: He still quacks.

DICKENS: We should all quack!

> *(ALL quack and laugh. DICKENS suddenly grabs his children up in a hug.)*

DICKENS: Children, we must never forget we are a one family of an even greater number.

KATE: What do you mean?

DICKENS: We are part of the family of man. We must love and care for each and every one of us. On this earth we are our brothers keeper, not just this season but also every day of the year.

BOZ: Do I have to always be nice?

DICKENS: Compassion—just find compassion, my son. There, but for the grace of God, go I.

MARY: You won't yell any more?

DICKENS: No, I promise.

CATHERINE: You seem in a better mood.

DICKENS: Darling, forgive me.

CATHERINE: I love you Charles.

DICKENS: And I you. Mrs. Dickens, you are Cleopatra to my Antony. You make me immortal.

(DICKENS kisses her.)

BOZ: Yuck!

(ALL laugh.)

CATHERINE: *(Coyly.)* Charles, what have you been writing?

DICKENS: Children, I am a changed man. From this Christmas onward, I promise never to be in a temper.

ALL: YEA!

DICKENS: I wasn't that bad, was I?

ALL: Yes!

BOZ: Read the story you've been working on?

DICKENS: Another time, let's spend this night together.

CATHERINE: Charles finish it. You're a writer and that aspiration was half the reason I fell in love with you.

DICKENS: I love you, Catherine.

CATHERINE: Children, let your father have a moment.

DICKENS: I'll be finished soon, my Queen.

CATHERINE: You do have a way with words, Mr. Dickens. This Christmas season, we've certainly seen the best of times and the worst of times.

DICKENS: Indeed.

CATHERINE: *(Exits, calling:)* Children, the Copperfield's should be here any moment.

DICKENS: "It was the best of times, it was the worst…" That is good—but let's save it for another story, shall we? *(HE writes.)* But Scrooge was early at the office next morning. Oh, he was early there. If he could only be there first, and catch Bob Cratchit coming late. That was the thing he had set his heart upon. And he did it; yes he did.
    (Shift: A clock begins chiming, SCROOGE is revealed in his office.)
The clock struck nine. No Bob. A quarter past. No Bob. He was full eighteen minutes and a half, behind his time.

    (DICKENS exits as CRATCHIT enters.)

SCROOGE: Cratchit! What do you mean by coming here

at this time of day.

CRATCHIT: I am very sorry, sir, I am behind my time.

SCROOGE: Indeed you are.

CRATCHIT: Its only once a year, sir. It shall not be repeated. I was making rather merry yesterday, sir.

SCROOGE: *(Brandishing his cane.)* Step this way.

CRATCHIT: Please, Mr. Scrooge.

SCROOGE: I warned you—

CRATCHIT: I have a family, sir—

SCROOGE: I am not going to stand this sort of thing any longer.

CRATCHIT: Lord, help me!

SCROOGE: Therefore—THEREFORE...I am about to raise your salary!

CRATCHIT: What?

SCROOGE: A merry Christmas, Bob! A merrier Christmas, my good fellow, than I have given you for many a year. I'll raise your salary and endeavor to assist your struggling family. Lets discuss it this very afternoon over a Christmas bowl of smoking bishop! Make up the fires and buy another coalscuttle before you dot another 'i,' Bob Cratchit.

(Shift: DICKENS is at his desk within his writing

circle. The FAMILY can be heard singing off stage. HE listens for a moment and then continues writing. After a time HE lays down his pen and savors his creation.)

DICKENS: Scrooge was better than his word. *(SCROOGE is revealed.)* He did it all, and infinitely more.

(TIM runs to SCROOGE and is swept up. THEY hold in an embrace.)

DICKENS: And to Tiny Tim, who did not die, he was a second father. He became as good a friend, as good a master and as good a man, as the good old city knew.

(The family song ends and the lights fade on all but DICKENS.)

DICKENS: Scrooge had no further intercourse with Spirits and it was always said of him, that he knew how to keep Christmas well, if any man alive possessed the knowledge. May that be truly said of all of us. And so, as Tiny Tim observed…God bless us. God bless us, every one.

(On the desk is a snow globe, DICKENS lifts the the globe and turns it over. It begins to snow on stage as the lights fade.)

END

www.ingramcontent.com/pod-product-compliance
Lightning Source LLC
Chambersburg PA
CBHW070133100426
42744CB00009B/1815